How to Adult

An illustrated guide

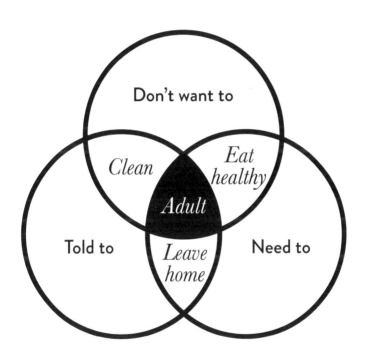

Don't want to

Clean

Eat healthy

Adult

Told to

Leave home

Need to

Stephen Wildish

POP PRESS

I can't even...

Adulting (*verb*): To do grown-up things and hold responsibilities such as having a job, paying rent or doing laundry. A verb used exclusively by those who adult less than 50 per cent of the time.

———————————

Contents

Introduction

Introduction

What does it mean to be an adult? When are you an adult? How can I adult? How can I possibly get to the end of this page without checking social media?

To be an adult, physically, is to be a person who is fully grown or developed. To be an adult socially is to be financially self-reliant (to have a job), to be independent (to not live with your parents) and responsible (to be able to make sensible decisions).

Legally you are an adult at eighteen, but adulthood can be a state of mind. There are kids out there running their own companies. They are adulting better than you.

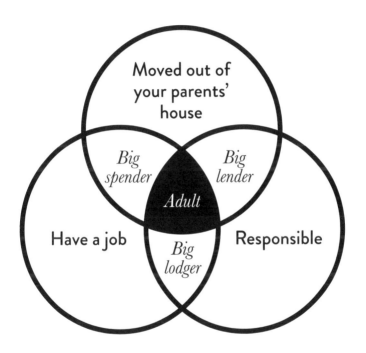

Teenage takes longer

To understand why some people can't adult anymore, let's look at a brief history of teenage years:

1850s: Average life expectancy in 1850 was around forty and childhood was short and sweet. Becoming an adult quickly was essential to avoid an even earlier grave.

1950s: The birth of teenagers. After five years of bebopping and skiffling their greased-up mopeds, 1950s teenagers knew it was time to grow up.

Now: We see the phenomenon of teenage years spreading out, with people in their late twenties who still have no idea what fabric conditioner is or how to adequately season a risotto.

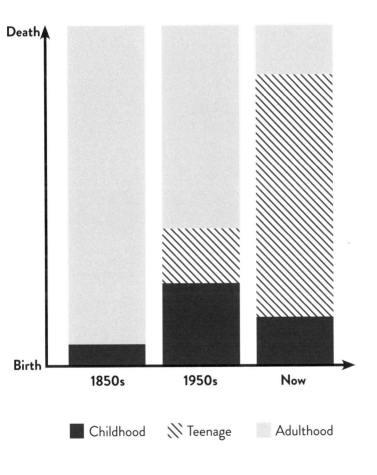

Biggest lies we tell ourselves

#1

JUST ONE MORE EPISODE

Biggest lies we tell ourselves

#2

JUST ONE MORE SLICE OF PIZZA

Can you adult today?

N   Y

Meh

Let's do this!

You've taken the first step to adulting and you've realised
you don't know how to do anything useful.

Let's look at how real adults do their adulting:

1. Controlling their emotions
They have the ability to cope with tricky situations rationally
and all without losing their shit.

2. Having goals
They have aims in life that are more than merely achieving high scores
on games and getting the 'squad' together for 'bants'. A key goal for
adults is to simply remember their 'bag for life' when they go shopping.

3. Being assertive
They find solutions to problems even when they
just want to sit in their pyjamas and watch daytime TV.

4. Making wise choices
These could be important financial decisions but could
also be as simple as deciding to go to bed at a decent time.

5. Keeping things tidy
They do laundry, clean the house and keep their personal
hygiene in a state that means their body doesn't resemble
an abandoned allotment.

Hierarchy of adulting activities

We will need to take baby steps if we are to succeed at adulting. After reading this book you might not necessarily be able to doff your unicorn onesie and emerge into the world in charge of the Bank of England, but here's hoping that you might be able to get out of bed and finally eat a salad.

The pinnacle for an adult seems to be talking to other adults about the intricacies of tracker mortgages, the ins and outs of stamp duty charges, and many other unfathomable things.

You simple fool! You don't know the difference between your equity and your accrual, do you?

Getting out of bed

Not eating pizza every day

Going to work

Surviving until payday

Talking about mortgages

More adult

Wanting to be a child

When things get tough, most of us feel a desire for others to take charge, to be dependent once again as we were in childhood. When we can no longer cope with the adult world, we often retreat to our beds, lose control and throw our toys out of the pram.

If it all goes wrong you could end up hiding in the shed for the afternoon or drinking gin through a straw.

But if you want to achieve things, make things happen or make sense of the adult world then you will need to grow up. Put down your phone, get off YouTube and pull yourself together: we are going to learn to adult.

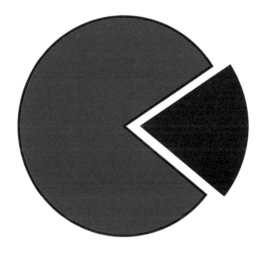

Non-adults who
see Pac-Man

Adults who
see a pie chart

Getting your shit together

It's time to dust yourself down, forget past attempts
to be an adult and get a plan together.

But it's not just getting your shit together, it's keeping it together
or you could quickly lose your shit (and then you will be in the shit).

To get your shit together, you need to make some life changes.
Let's not go crazy and sign up for a marathon. Start small,
tidy a few things, wear clean clothes. We can work up
to that marathon in good time.

The longer you can keep your shit together, the better
chance you have of making it in the adult world.

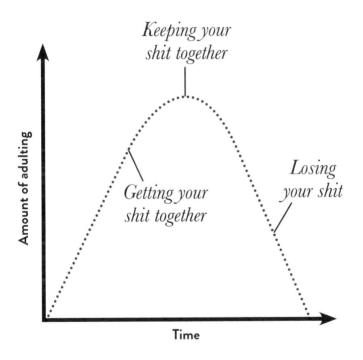

Chapter 1
Bed

Bed

Bed is a love-hate place for people trying to adult. At night they can't be coaxed into it and in the morning they can't be coaxed out. Living like this means they never get their full eight hours sleep. A good night's sleep can mean the difference between a successful day and the kind of day that leaves you hiding under the blankets.

For adults, weeks are divided up into 'school nights' and weekends. A 'school night' means any night where you have to be awake and responsible at an early hour. For example on a 'school night' it is not advisable to go to the pub. It is much safer to stay at home with a cup of cocoa and get an early night.

Getting into bed

Adults have a set bedtime. They choose to
go to bed rather than stay up to do fun things.

When you're in bed, your body is usually tired, but your mind can
be a funfair of thoughts; although phones and tablets can distract
you from your worries, they also don't help you get to sleep. It's
very easy to binge on episodes of the latest Nordic crime thriller
or simply sit watching amusing cat videos until 3 a.m.

You know you have a problem when your device begins
to judge you for watching five episodes in a row.

What your device says	What your device means
'Are you still watching?'	'Bloody hell, you need to stop watching!'

Getting out of bed

To successfully get out of bed, firstly you need to get out of bed.
The main hurdle to getting out of bed is not being asleep. Setting
multiple alarms works for some, placing an alarm clock in a drawer away
from the bed works for others. Just stay away from that snooze button.

If you have managed to prise yourself from your bed, it is now time to
make your bed! It's a great way to set yourself up for the sort of positive
day that would put Mary Poppins to shame. It only takes a few minutes
but means that your first task of the day is completed. Tick!

Biggest lies we tell ourselves

#3

I'LL GO TO BED EARLY TONIGHT

Biggest lies we tell ourselves

#4

I'LL GET UP EARLY TOMORROW

Adult sleep pattern

Characterised by a nice early bedtime and going straight to sleep. Briskly rising with the alarm call, followed by a day of twenty-four carat adulting.

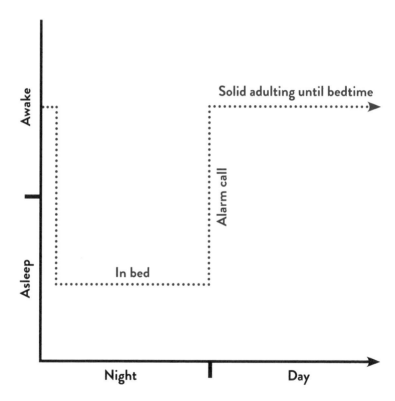

Non-adult sleep pattern

Characterised by slouching on the sofa watching boxsets at 1.30 a.m. with no intention of going to bed. Slowly coming around by midday to catch up on daytime TV. A mid-afternoon nap, then back to slouching.

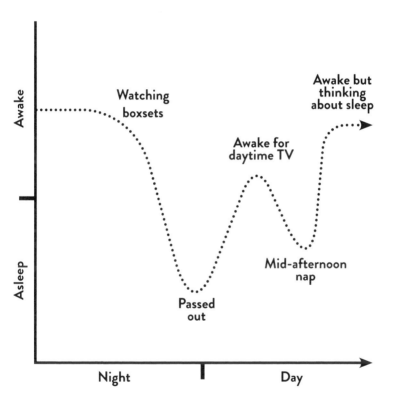

Napping

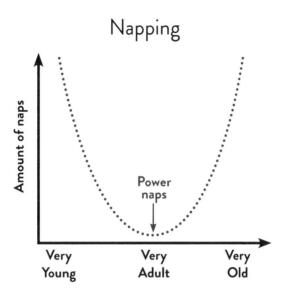

Naps are short periods of sleep taken during the day. It's very common for children or old people to nap, but most adults tend to take few or no naps. The major exception to the rule is after a Sunday roast, when the irresistible 'cloak of napping' descends upon the adult brain.

Another way adults can nap is if they call it a 'power nap'. This sounds like you are still being productive. Napping in this manner can actually be beneficial, as a nap that lasts around thirty minutes can boost brain function and leave you feeling restored. But a longer nap can mean slipping into a deep sleep and really fucking up your day.

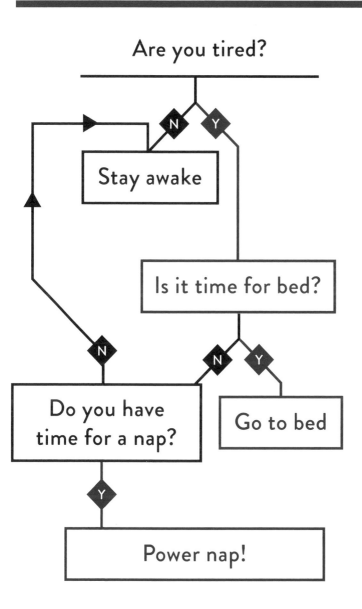

Are you tired?

Stay awake

Is it time for bed?

Do you have time for a nap?

Go to bed

Power nap!

Chapter 2
Work

Work

Holding down regular employment is essential for adult life. It means you can be financially independent from others and able to fund the fun things you like to do at the weekend.

If you can find a job that pays well and that you enjoy, you've hit the jackpot. If not then you will have to endure the working week like the rest of us.

Getting a job

A job interview is one of the most stressful experiences a person who is pretending to adult can go through. It's basically a test to see how adult you are. Remember to be yourself, unless 'yourself' is an idiot, in which case try to be someone normal.

You will be asked to answer questions like 'What are your strengths?' Try to offer positive adult answers like, 'I'm a hard-working team player and I love a challenge.' Under no circumstances should you tell them that you can eat seven hot dogs in under a minute. It's impressive but just not what they are after.

Conversely, if you are asked about your weaknesses try to offer a positive spin: 'I sometimes work too hard and I'm a bit of a perfectionist.' Obviously don't tell them that you pick your nose and smell your farts, you disgusting animal.

Don't say	Do say
I am pretty much unskilled	I am keen to learn
Can I use the bog?	Apologies, may I take five minutes?
What do you do here again?	Can you tell me more about your industry?
How do you feel about duvet days?	Are there flexible working hours?
I'm great at stealing stuff	I'm resourceful
I can't stop fucking swearing	Creative language is one of my key skills
What?!	Can you repeat the question?

Commuting

Getting to and from work requires a coping strategy all of its own. Public transport can be noisy, smelly and uncomfortable, plus you will be avoiding interaction with general members of the public, fellow commuters, and perverts (sometimes one and the same).

If you commute by car, you can use the additional time in your vehicle to psych yourself up before you have to interact with adults. For safety reasons, don't use this time to do your make-up in the rear-view mirror, or to eat your breakfast (especially if it's cereal and milk in a bowl).

However you travel, get to know the journey time. Leave enough time to get to work with ten minutes to spare. Being predictably late every day with no real excuse is not a great look.

Coping strategies for a commute on public transport include:

Headphones
These form a physical barrier between you and the outside world. Listen to calming music, a self-help audiobook or just white noise.

Read the paper
Choose something intelligent. Don't worry, they all have cartoons.

'Working' on your laptop
Pretend to do crucial work on a laptop, while actually playing solitaire. Writing gibberish in a Word document makes you look important.

Talking to other commuters
Obviously not, this was put here to see if you are still paying attention.

Drinking
On train journeys, adults can drink coffee on the journey in and booze on the journey home, never the other way around!

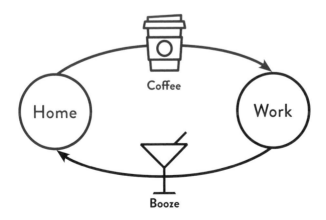

How should you get to work?

Feeling energetic?

N   **Y**

Does your work have showers?

Does public transport go there?

N   **Y**

Public transport

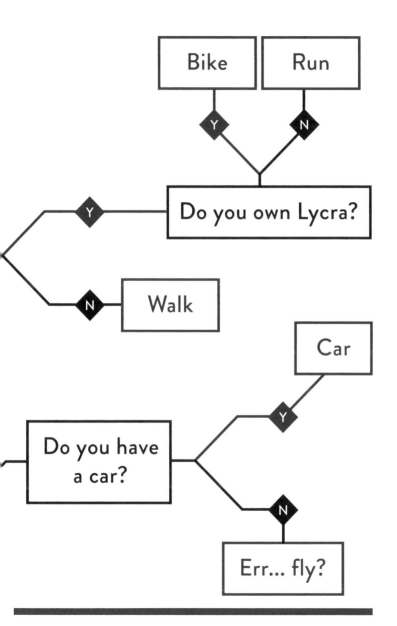

Keeping a job

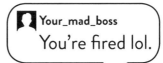

John_buckysesh69

My boss is a mad old knob lol!

Your_mad_boss

You're fired lol.

It's a good idea to try to retain employment at all times, even if your current work situation isn't ideal. It shows perseverance and dedication to future employers. Also regular pay cheques are good for your work–life balance.

1. Don't call the boss a knob
They probably are a knob, but there's no need to start telling the truth at work.

2. Make drinks
Offer to make teas and coffees for the team. It looks like a selfless act of generosity, but you know it's simply time away from your desk.

3. Do the work
Do the work that you are supposed to do. Don't do the work you are not supposed to do or, even worse, don't not do any work at all.

Work–life balance

As you get more adult you will drift from the 'too much play' zone through to 'too much work'. A healthy balance of the two will see you maintaining your adultness for longer.

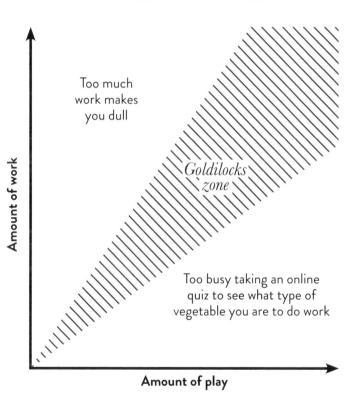

Too much
work makes
you dull

Goldilocks zone

Too busy taking an online
quiz to see what type of
vegetable you are to do work

Amount of work

Amount of play

Workplace talk

Workplaces have their own vocabulary and it will be beneficial
to learn some of the phrases you will hear from people around you.

One variation of office talk you will come across is 'management speak'.
This is language that is needlessly complex, filled with jargon and that
neither the speaker nor the listener fully understand. Be warned, it's
good to understand the basics, but don't start to talk like this. It cannot
be overstated that people who use management speak are arseholes.

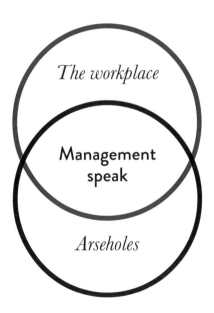

What they say	What they mean
Have your ducks in a row	Get organised
Blue sky thinking	Think about something
Let's touch base offline	I want to talk
Run this up the flagpole	Let's see if this idea is good
Low hanging fruit	Complete easy tasks
Let's not boil the ocean here, if we synergise the process and look under the bonnet we won't have to punch the puppy. It's win-win!	Fuck knows?

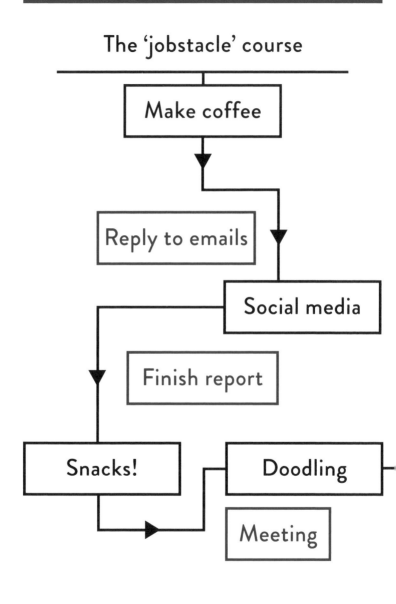

The 'jobstacle' course

Make coffee

Reply to emails

Social media

Finish report

Snacks!

Doodling

Meeting

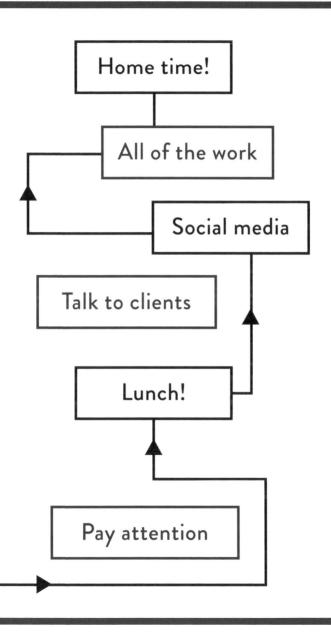

Meetings

Meetings are 99 per cent a waste of everyone's time. They are called by people who can't make decisions and want to feel important. Normally a meeting will conclude with nothing accomplished and people leaving more confused than they were before.

So how do you get through a pointless meeting?

1. Take notes
It's important to note things down periodically to make it look as if you are listening. It doesn't matter what you write, you will never refer to these notes. If you do doodle, try not to get caught drawing a cock and balls, however tempting this is.

2. Nod your head
Nod your head periodically to let people know you are listening (even when you clearly are not).

3. Stay alert
Keep your body language positive, don't fold your arms or close your eyes. There is a chance you could be asked a question at any time. Try to keep track of what pointless thing is being discussed and have at least one thoughtful comment to make.

Meeting time breakdown

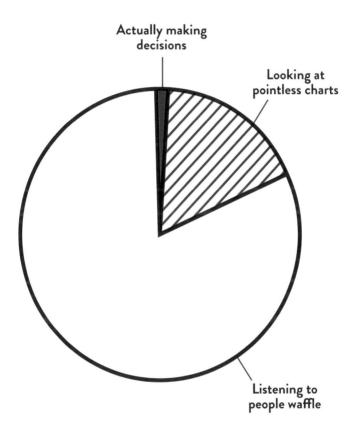

Actually making decisions

Looking at pointless charts

Listening to people waffle

How to adult at work

REPLACE

FUCK YOU

WITH OKAY GREAT

Should I call in sick?

Are you sick?

N Y

Go to work

Call in sick

Pulling a sickie

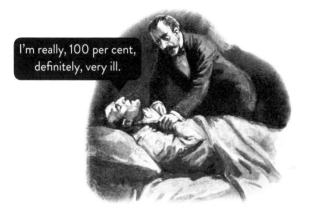

I'm really, 100 per cent, definitely, very ill.

In extreme circumstances it may become necessary to 'pull a sickie'. Which involves tricking your work into thinking you have a mystery illness that lasts the same amount of time as the working day.

There are some basic ground rules:

1. Always phone in sick
Never email your workplace to let them know you are 'sick'. An email or text is the tool of the inexperienced and will get you fired.

2. Don't leave the house or post on social media
You will be spotted somehow, by someone.

Keeping your shit together

Most of the working day is spent keeping your shit together. If your computer crashes and you lose a whole morning's unsaved work, what do you do? Keep your shit together.

Having a tantrum or crying in the stationery cupboard is going to affect your career progression. You need to show stability and positivity at work.

Coping tips to help keep your shit together:

1. Breathe
If you just want to scream, take a moment, count to ten and breathe slowly. It might just stop you saying something you regret.

2. Vent
Find a safe place to vent your frustrations. Avoid email, as it's far too easy to hit 'reply all' and get yourself in hot water with the entire company. Far better to find a trusted colleague and vent over a coffee.

When you get home from a hard day's
adulting and can finally be yourself again.

Chapter 3
Social Media

Social Media

In this modern age most of our lives and interactions are played out online, in social media or through email and text message.

People use social media to present the best possible version of themselves to the world. Instagram photos can be selected, edited and filtered to within an inch of their lives.

As you sit merrily typing your latest update into Facebook, it is easy to lose sight of the audience of people out there who might be reading what you type. Of course there is a greater chance that no one really cares.

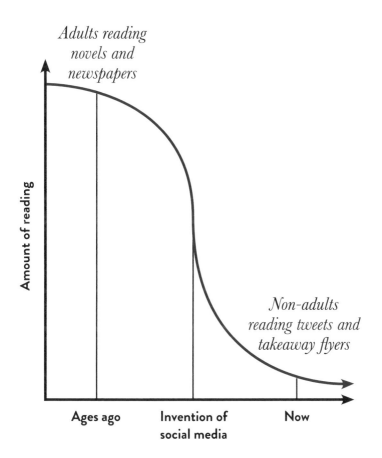

Social media explained:

EAGERLY RECORDING YOURSELF...

...ACHIEVING ABSOLUTELY NOTHING

Social media addiction

Staring blankly at your phone refreshing a feed of memes can affect your mental health. On social media people show us their best lives, their wonderful holidays and their glamorous new toilet paper and this can cause you to feel envy and self-loathing. Your toilet paper is probably just normal, isn't it?

Many non-adults find themselves checking their phones every ten seconds, no matter what situation they find themselves in, sometimes even mid-conversation...

Should I check my phone?

Is it more than thirty minutes since you last checked?

N   Y

Sure, check your phone

Social media by average user

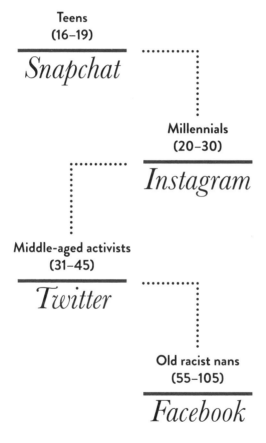

**Teens
(16–19)**

Snapchat

**Millennials
(20–30)**

Instagram

**Middle-aged activists
(31–45)**

Twitter

**Old racist nans
(55–105)**

Facebook

Oversharing on social media

On social media it is incredibly easy to overshare
and give out too much information.

Most people have no desire to see another poorly lit photo of your
dreadful dinner or your fourteenth Minion meme of the day. Try to limit
holiday posts and photos. Place all your photos in one album so people
can choose to avoid seeing every single cocktail you drank over the space
of two weeks. Not everything you do needs to be seen or heard.

Similarly, if you are in a relationship, the occasional 'I love you' posts to
one another are sickening but acceptable. The sign of a good, healthy
relationship is that there is no sign of it on social media.

Remember it's a status, not a diary.

Platform	What non-adults use it for	What adults use it for
Facebook	Minion memes	Updates about family and friends
Twitter	Trolling celebrities	Complaining to brands about poor service
Instagram	Filtered selfies with bunny ears	Pictures of holidays
Snapchat	Dick pics	[not used by adults]
Pinterest	[not used by non-adults]	Pictures of candles and home furnishings

Vaguebooking

Vaguebooking is a phenomenon that involves simultaneously sharing too much and not enough. It's a status update that is intentionally vague, leaving out crucial pieces of information to keep people guessing and to give the poster more 'mystique'.

We all have that friend whose typical vaguebook status would be 'I don't want to talk about it', 'Is it worth it?', 'Not naming any names but...' or passive-aggressively checking into hospital. They are looking for attention or compliments.

Adults don't vaguebook. If you are in need of attention and are experiencing real anguish, close Facebook and speak to someone in the real world over a drink.

Should I respond to a vaguebook?

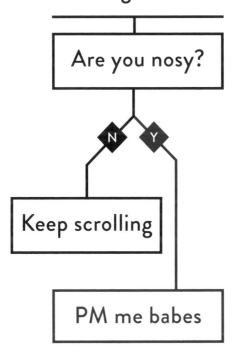

Are you nosy?

N

Y

Keep scrolling

PM me babes

Should I send a dick pic?

Have they asked for it?

N →

Y → **Really?**

N →

Y → **Come on, seriously?**

N →

Y → **Double check**

Don't send a dick pic

Sending nudes

Adults do not send nude photos of themselves to other people. Adults know that, once out of your control, these images can be shared everywhere and will last for ever. If you are asked for nudes, think long and hard, much like the pervert who asked for the nudes.

If you do insist on sending out photos of your privates, make sure your face is not in them, so you can at least claim anonymity when they are inevitably leaked at a later date.

Lastly, if your picture has not been asked for, do not send it. That is a cast-iron rule not to be broken.

Should I post this status?

Is it about your dinner?

N   Y

No

N   Y

Would you tell your friend if you met them?

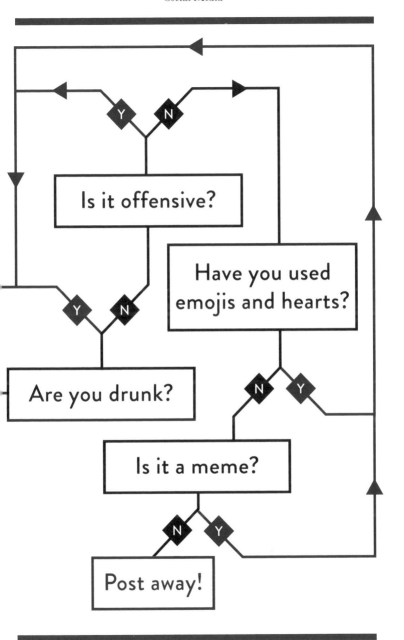

Chapter 4

Household Tasks

Household Tasks

Completing tasks around the house is base-level adulting. Everything from tidying up after yourself to washing clothes and dishes. Break out the duster and be prepared to get a mop involved, we are going to do some chores!

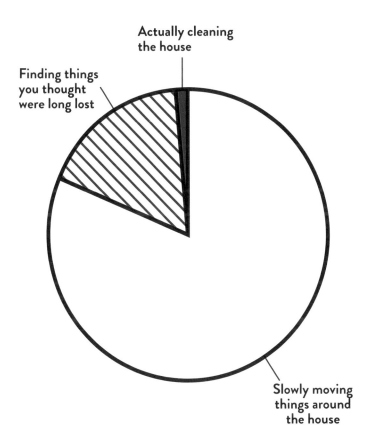

Actually cleaning
the house

Finding things
you thought
were long lost

Slowly moving
things around
the house

Loading the dishwasher

Since the first caveman fried the first rasher of bacon, humans have washed the dishes. Now, if you are very, very lucky you might have access to a most powerful technological wonder: The Dishwasher.

A whole book could be written about correct placement of kitchenware in the dishwasher but as a rough guide:

Glasses and bowls
Glasses go in the top drawer. Bowls are a wild card and can go in the top or bottom drawer.

Knives
Knives and sharp implements are placed blade down to avoid a grisly accident. Table knives can be placed blade up along with forks and spoons for optimal cleaning.

Pots, pans and plates
Plates and pans go in the bottom drawer along with the cutlery basket. Rinse off the larger bits of food waste in the sink before loading into the dishwasher.

Detergent
Never, ever use washing-up liquid in the dishwasher thinking you've discovered a great life hack.
Trust me on this. Always use dishwasher-specific detergents or capsules.

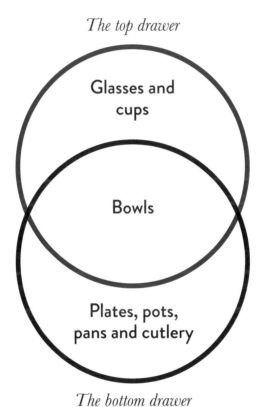

The top drawer

Glasses and cups

Bowls

Plates, pots, pans and cutlery

The bottom drawer

In the dishwasher:

KNIVES DOWN

FORKS UP

...that's the way we like to wash cutlery

Laundry

When your clothes, fabrics or teddy bears are dirty or smelly they need to be washed. A washing machine may look daunting but it is really quite simple:

1. Fill the machine with dirty clothes.

2. Don't mix colours and whites.

3. Select the wash you need.

If in doubt, select a low temperature eco wash, as disasters such as shrinkage or colour leakage are less likely at lower temperatures.

4. Remove and dry the clothes when the cycle is finished.

Instead of leaving your soggy washing on a drying rack for three weeks, you can use a tumble dryer if you have one or, if you're feeling wholesome, hang it outside on a washing line.

Clothes have handy symbols on the label that tell you how to wash and care for the item:

Wash at 40°C

Never wash

X-Men clothes

Washing machine is watching you

Curling is allowed

NO CURLING!

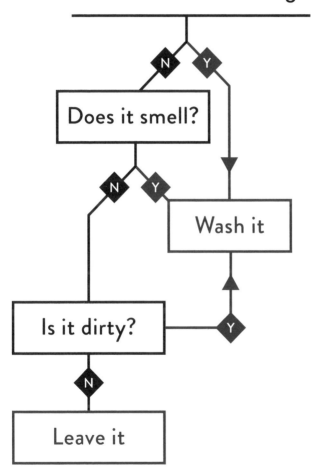

Does this need washing?

Does it smell?

Wash it

Is it dirty?

Leave it

Toilet roll

Even children can use toilet roll to wipe their bottoms,
so thankfully we don't need to go into that here. Do we?
What we *do* need to discuss is the correct way
the toilet roll should sit on the holder.

The roll is placed so the next piece of paper is in the 'over' position
and it is offered to you in front of the roll. The 1891 patent for the
toilet roll details that this is the correct way.

If the roll is placed in the 'under' position, so the paper
is sitting towards the wall, it's easy to scrape your hand on
the wall and harder to access the next piece of paper.

In defence of the 'under' position, it does make it harder for
children and cats to unspool the entire roll onto the floor.

I will ruin your day.

The correct 'over' position

The incorrect 'under' position

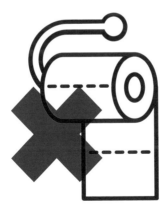

Recycling

Adults know to put out the recycling either weekly or bi-weekly. Household recycling is normally for paper, glass, metal and plastics. For larger items a 'tip trip' is required.

Glass
Explain the presence of all those bottles to the recycling man by pretending that you've had a party instead of having a borderline drinking problem.

Paper and metal

	Adult	Non-adult
Paper	Broadsheet newspapers	Pizza boxes
Metal	Tins of legumes	Beer cans

Tip trip
A tip trip is such an adult activity that when asked the question 'What are you up to this weekend?', you can answer with 'A tip trip,' and that can apparently account for your entire weekend.

If you are lucky, you can have a full thirty-minute conversation about how to time your visit to avoid the queues.

Should I recycle this?

Can it be recycled?

N   Y

Recycle it

Don't recycle it

Should I tidy this thing away?

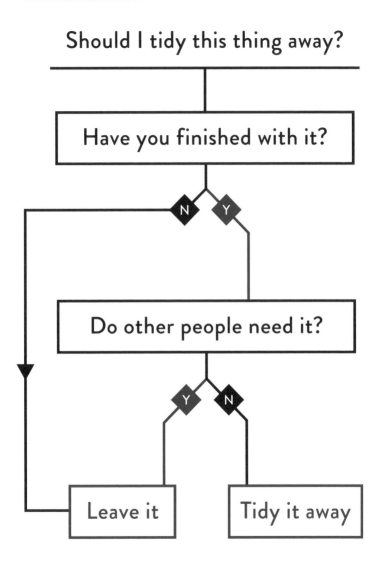

Have you finished with it?

N Y

Do other people need it?

Y N

Leave it   Tidy it away

Tidying

Adults desire a clutter-free environment in which to sit and do adult things like review insurance policies or read lofty novels.

To correctly adult, you need to clean up after yourself and, sometimes, others. Follow these tips for a neat and tidy life:

1. Put things away after you have used them
Things have a home where they live, so when you've finished with them put them back. Don't put empty cartons and packages back in the cupboard or fridge: they belong in the bin (see page 80 on recycling).

2. If you find things that are not tidy, tidy them
You may not have made the mess but as a responsible adult you should tidy things whenever you can.

Chapter 5
Grooming

Grooming

Being clean, presentable and smelling nice.
Not too much to ask is it? Well, apparently it is for you.

Thousands of scientists have worked tirelessly to bring you
wonder products like: boswelloxium, b-complex-activated charcoal
face masks and vitamin-enriched intimate douches. These marvels
of science make it easy to keep yourself clean.
And yet you still wash once a month with an old rag.

Shower time breakdown

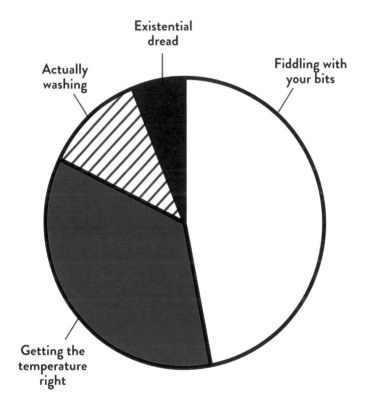

Existential
dread

Fiddling with
your bits

Actually
washing

Getting the
temperature
right

Male grooming

Adult men know that they need to smell nice, look presentable and be neatly trimmed. If you're spraying layers of deodorant on your soiled neck beard then you are not adulting correctly.

With bathing, adult men are not suckered in by the 'fragile masculinity' trend of adding macho ingredients to bubble bath to make them more 'manly'. A real adult man is happy to soak in a ' lavender bubble bath' and not a 'muscle soak with charcoal and nettles'.

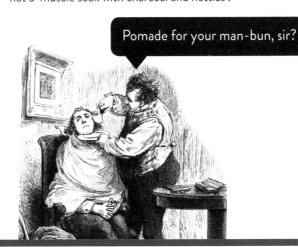

As a man you may be able to grow a fine, full adult beard or moustache. A certain level of grooming is to be expected with facial hair, as an unkempt, food-soaked beard is not desirable. If you do tend toward the wizard end of the spectrum, don't be surprised if you are regularly stopped and asked for three wishes.

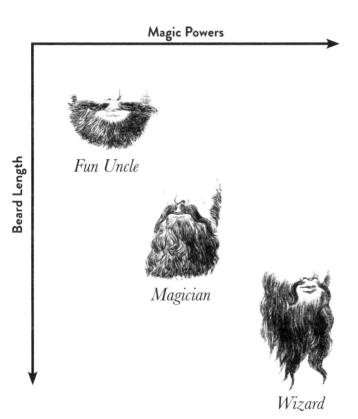

Magic Powers

Beard Length

Fun Uncle

Magician

Wizard

Female grooming

Make-up is fun. If you want to wear blue lipstick and fake eyelashes to go to the corner shop, go for it!

Just remember that if you don't want to wear make-up, that's fine too. And unless they are mermaids, unicorns or YouTube vloggers, real adults tend to steer clear of glitter on weekdays.

In any case, you want to avoid the 'tidemark' of foundation around the chin. Blending is your friend.

Remember, it's a face and not a colouring book.

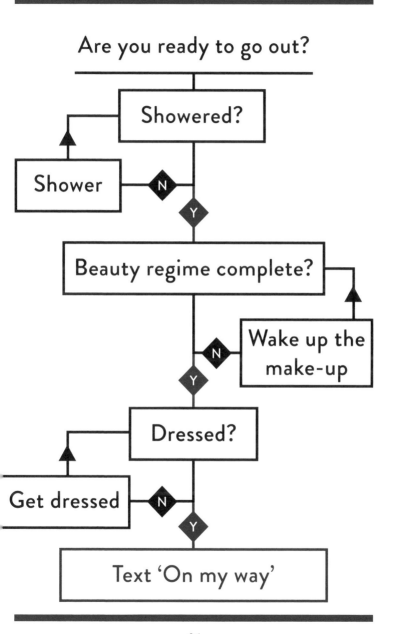

Are you ready to go out?

Showered?

Shower

N

Y

Beauty regime complete?

Wake up the make-up

N

Y

Dressed?

Get dressed

N

Y

Text 'On my way'

Oral hygiene

Cleaning your teeth twice a day is an essential
part of your daily routine. No excuses.

You will need to first floss your teeth
and then brush your teeth for about three minutes.

If you do manage to fit cleaning your teeth into your morning
and evening schedule you will be less scared of visiting your
dentist. You will no longer be forced to lie about how regularly
you brush your teeth.

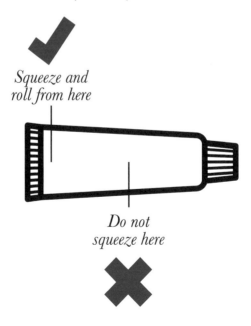

*Squeeze and
roll from here*

*Do not
squeeze here*

Amount of toothpaste

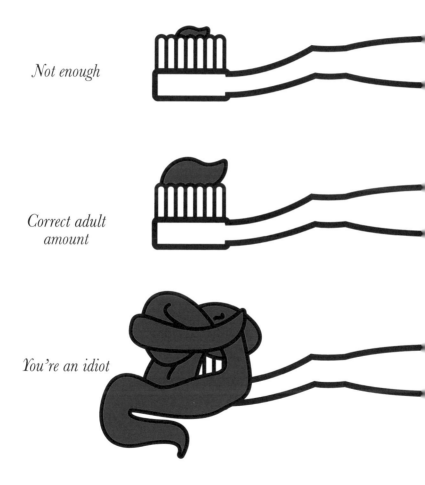

Not enough

*Correct adult
amount*

You're an idiot

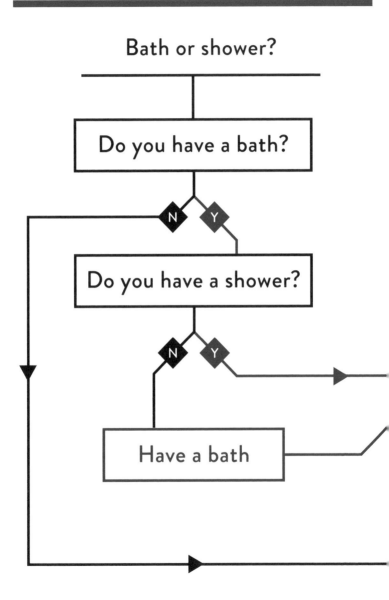

Bath or shower?

Do you have a bath?

N Y

Do you have a shower?

N Y

Have a bath

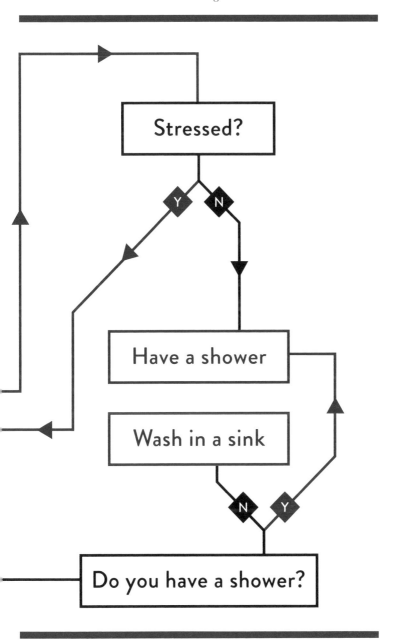

When you reach in your pocket just to check your phone is still there.

Reminder

This is your halfway reminder to put
your phone down and pay attention.

Chapter 6
Conversations

Conversations

Talking to other adults is tricky. They often talk about subjects you have little or no knowledge of, using big words like 'dichotomy' or 'hyperbole'. Which you had no idea were spelled like that, did you?

Be it in the workplace, at home or on the street, there is no getting away from it: adults will want to talk to you and you can't stare at the floor and pretend you didn't hear them for ever.

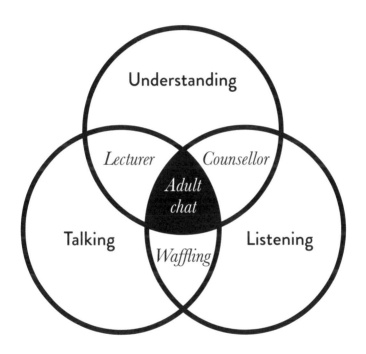

Small talk

Hi, how are you? I'm fine, thank you. Lovely weather, isn't it?

All examples of the terror of small talk. Tiny conversations with people we barely know and have no desire to know. But we can't tell them to fuck off because that would appear rude.

Instead, a simple way to get through small talk is to ask open-ended questions, i.e. nothing with a 'yes' or 'no' answer. Discuss the surroundings you are in, sports or a shared interest. Don't worry about silences; they are never as long as you imagine they are!

Small talk dos	Small talk don'ts
Be interested in the other person	Stare at your phone and mutter obscenities
Make eye contact	Look them in the eye, not blinking for over five minutes
Discuss shared interests	Talk about your extensive funeral plans
Comment on the weather	Comment on their shabby appearance
Give an appropriate greeting	Greet them with the middle finger
Say 'Nice to meet you'	Say 'Fuck off'

JUST
NOD

TO LET THEM KNOW YOU ARE LISTENING

Being polite

Being polite shows a level of compassion and understanding of other people's feelings, something a teenager or non-adult lacks. Being polite is an ability to use the words 'please', 'thank you', 'sorry' and 'excuse me' when relevant. If in doubt, throw a 'sorry' in there.

In conversations with adults, it is polite to ask how the other person is. This isn't actually a request for information and if you are asked how you are, you should not give the correct information.
Just respond with 'Fine, thanks.'

Should I say sorry?

Was it your fault?

N   Y

Say sorry

Me after a long day of
pretending to be polite

Using the telephone

Using the telephone to call people you don't know is a
high-stress situation for someone who isn't able to adult.
Will you say the wrong thing? Will your voice be squeaky?
Will you call them 'Mum' accidentally?

Many people avoid phone conversations completely and rely on text
or email as a solution to communication needs. However, as an adult,
for purposes of clarity and speed, sometimes you just have to brace
yourself and pick up the phone.

To get through the call you can:

1. Rehearse
What do you want to say?
What do you want from the call?

2. Breathe
Take some deep breaths
to calm your nerves.

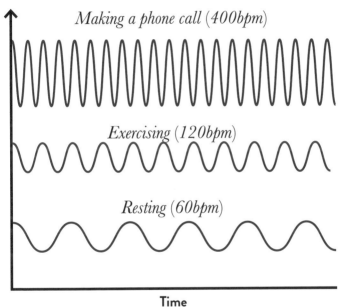

Biggest lies we tell others

#1

I'M ON MY WAY

Biggest lies we tell others

#2

I'M
FINE

When you text someone but they call you back

Texting

Text messages are an informal way to communicate with friends and family and are perfect for sending a quick note or update. Don't use texts for formal conversations or to send bad news (e.g. 'Your nans dead m8').

Make sure when you are texting that:

1. You are texting the right person
Sending your mum photos of your genitals is considered a major social faux pas.

2. Autocorrect doesn't make you look foolish
'A nap' can autocorrect to 'anal' with hilarious consequences.

Should I call or text?

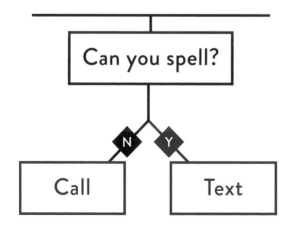

Can you spell?

N — Call

Y — Text

Chapter 8
Finances

Finances

Can you be trusted to make financial decisions when you still have to sing the alphabet in your head to get to the right letter?

Finances, mortgages and pensions are like quantum physics: unfathomable and best left to boffins to work out the nitty gritty. It is, however, a good idea to have a basic grasp of the financial concepts you will need in your adult life.

Buy all the things?

Do you have savings?

No

Surviving until payday

Budgets are important to adults. They will help you ensure even spending across the month and avoid lean times before payday. In lean times you discover new and creative cookery skills just to survive. Top tip: stuffing mix and gravy powder can make a delicious dinner for two.

As a guide you should be budgeting 50 per cent of your wages for things you need, 30 per cent for things you want and 20 per cent towards savings.

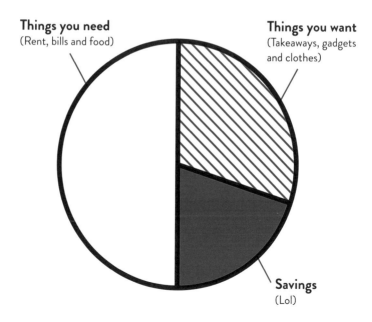

Things you need
(Rent, bills and food)

Things you want
(Takeaways, gadgets and clothes)

Savings
(Lol)

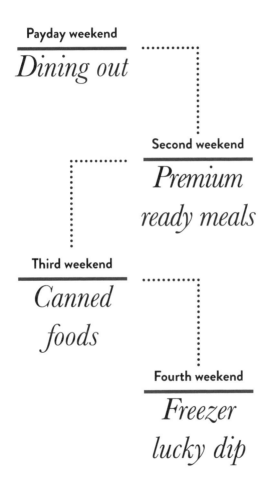

Payday weekend

Dining out

Second weekend

Premium ready meals

Third weekend

Canned foods

Fourth weekend

Freezer lucky dip

Week of payday

Rest of the month

Paying bills

Bills are the reason you have to go to work, and are to be respected. You can't just ignore them and hope they will go away.

With the correct budget and planning, you can pay bills when they are due *and* have more than £1.26 left over to survive the rest of the month.

It's good practice to review bills and payments that you make, as companies might try to add extra charges or charge you for things you didn't sign up for.

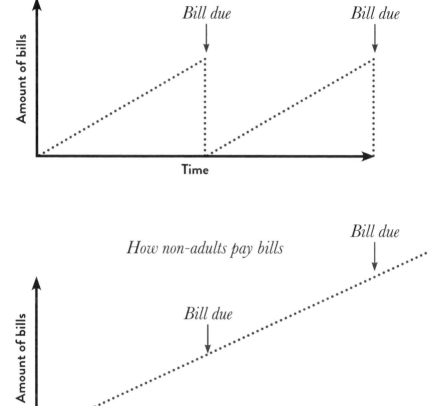

How adults pay bills

MONEY
DOESN'T MAKE
YOU HAPPY...

BUT IT IS MORE COMFORTABLE CRYING IN A MANSION

Mortgages and pensions

At some point in your life you may be in a position where you have to consider getting a mortgage or a pension. Both of these things require financial planning and understanding.

If you visit a financial planner, they will explain to you in explicit detail that on your current savings plan, when you retire you will be able to live comfortably for about thirteen minutes before you're thrown into a debtors' prison. So, good luck with that.

The sooner you start saving the better.

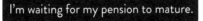

Financial word	What is it?
Pension	Money you give to the bank in the hope they will give it back to you. With a bit extra
Mortgage	Money the bank gives you in the hope you will give it back to them. With a bit extra
Life insurance	Money the bank gives your dependants if you get hit by a bus
Life assurance	Money the bank gives you if you don't get hit by a bus
Stocks and shares	Made-up money being moved around. You will need a pinstripe suit and red braces to understand this

Making financial decisions

Decisions about money are a battle between
your rational side and your impulsive side.

If you let your impulsive side take control, you will
end up with no money and a house full of junk.
If rationality prevails, you almost never get to have fun.

Your bank
account

I'm going out this weekend.

Do you need this thing?

N Y

Don't buy it

Can you afford it?

N Y

Is it the cheapest available?

N Y

Buy it!

Chapter 9
Food

Food

Adults eat balanced meals at regular times; they don't have 2 a.m. fish finger sandwiches or bowls of cereal for lunch. Sensible and balanced eating is key to the adult lifestyle. Chocolate is not breakfast.

Adding vegetables to your plate and removing the food cooked in breadcrumbs is a great place to start. Get up close and personal with an aubergine, greet a beet.

The shop didn't have any porcini risotto so I've replaced it all with toast.

Eating in company

When in company, it's best to eat your food in a calm and controlled manner with as little noise and mess as possible.

If you take your packed lunch out at work and your co-workers flee their desks, it's usually a good pointer that this area needs work. If you struggle with slurping noises, it is wise to avoid foods like spaghetti and soup.

Pasta dishes by 'adultness'

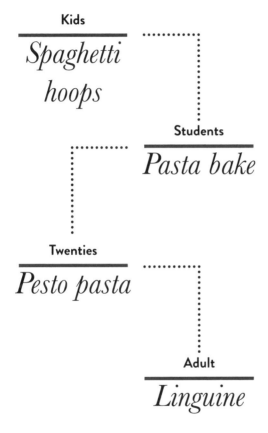

Kids

Spaghetti hoops

Students

Pasta bake

Twenties

Pesto pasta

Adult

Linguine

Dinner parties

Adults have dinner parties. They invite over some friends that they secretly despise for an evening of moderate drinking and pretentious food.

Throwing a dinner party

Plan a meal that means you spend the least amount of time in the kitchen, unless you don't really like the guests. In that case, the kitchen is a good place to hide.

Plan three courses of sophisticated food. Ready meals or anything from a can won't cut it. You can buy dessert, but rough up the edges with a knife to make it look 'home-made'.

Don't get drunk before the guests turn up.

This is
called fruit

Attending a dinner party

Bring a gift, but choose carefully. Flowers can cause a fuss when the host has to fetch a vase. Wine is a much safer bet, although there is the danger of bringing red to a fish-based meal and looking like a complete fool. Don't bring a bottle of strong cider or spirits, you're not on the 'sesh' tonight.

Eat the food provided without complaining. Any dietary requirements should have been submitted beforehand. If steak tartare is on the menu and you are not a fan, then get your best pretending face on. You've got a long meal ahead of you.

Keep conversation light and appropriate. Nobody wants to hear about your awful job or your genital warts, or even your awful job in the genital wart clinic.

EAT MORE GREENS

EAT LESS BEIGE

The pudding and responsibilities correlation

A clear indicator that you are not adulting is eating too many sweet treats. Children expect pudding with every meal, but as you gain responsibilities and independence your dessert dependence drops off. However, when old age hits and your responsibilities begin to wane, the desserts are back on the menu!

Children are often told that fruit and yoghurt are in fact pudding, when we know all too well that they are nothing but garnishes to the real thing. Now you are adulting, you will have to decide when to eat pudding and when to have fruit instead.

Fruit is one of my five a day. Chocolate cake is the other four.

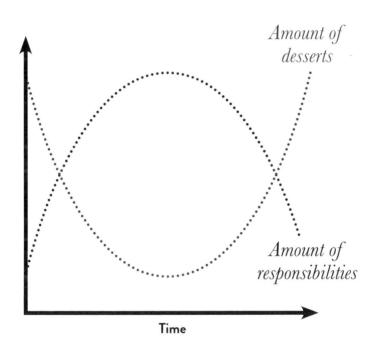

Amount of desserts

Amount of responsibilities

Time

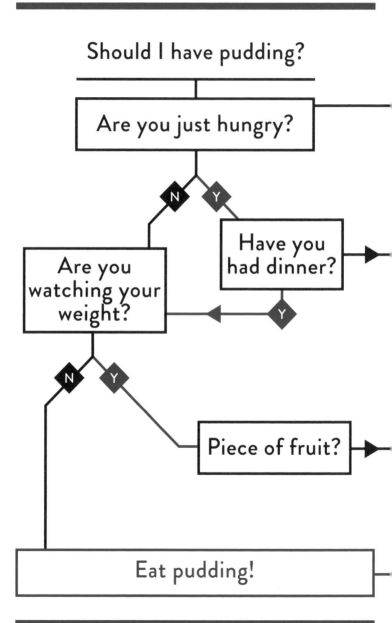

Should I have pudding?

Are you just hungry?

N | Y

Have you had dinner?

Y

Are you watching your weight?

N | Y

Piece of fruit?

Eat pudding!

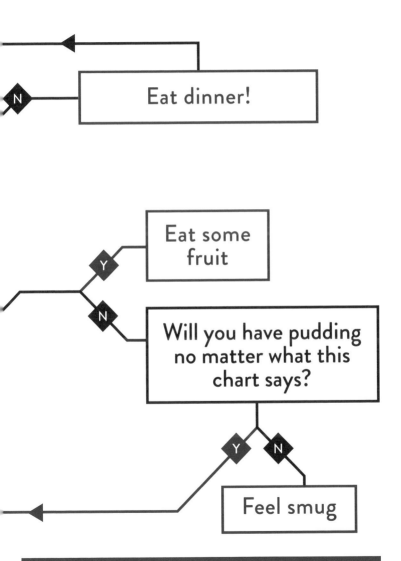

Me:

THE DIET STARTS TOMORROW

Also me:

CAKE ISN'T GOING TO EAT ITSELF, IS IT?

Eating healthily

Eating a balanced diet is exactly that, a balance.
Everything in moderation. If you are looking to lose weight don't
go in for fad diets. Just eat a little less and move a bit more.

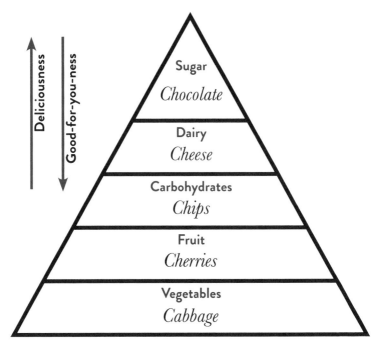

If you're looking at the chart above and think you now have to
eat a cabbage-cherry casserole then you need to read a few cook
books and stay off the cheesy chips for a while.

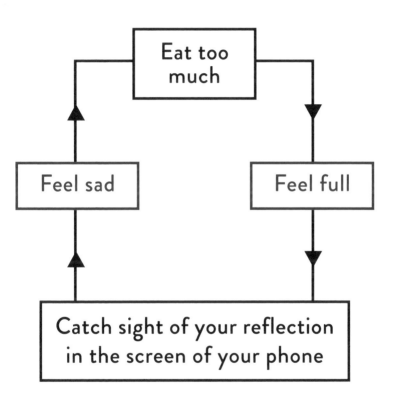

Should I get a takeaway?

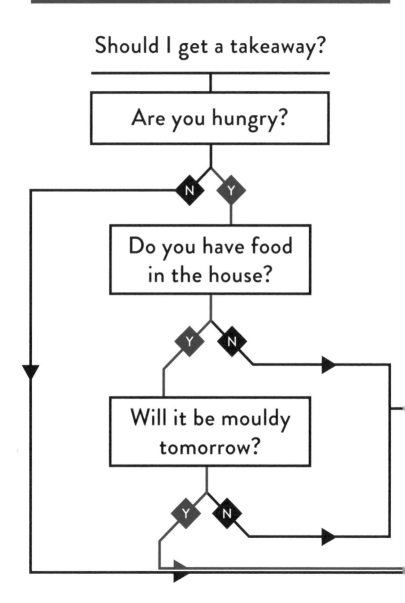

Are you hungry?

N Y

Do you have food in the house?

Y N

Will it be mouldy tomorrow?

Y N

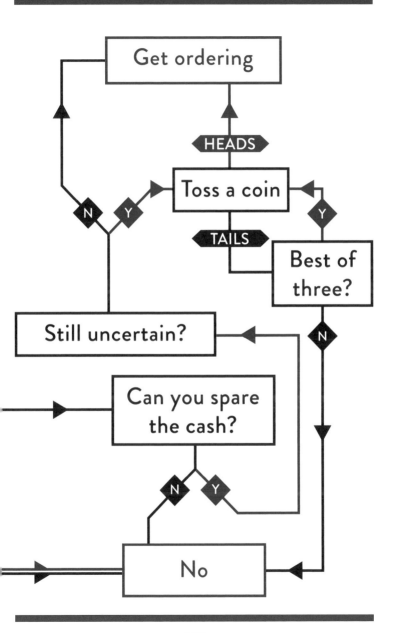

Chapter 10
Drink

Drink

Adults appreciate wine and sip fine brandy. There's no quicker way to show that you are not adult than to down your drink, order shots and end up losing control of your bladder in a taxi home.

Adults pretend to only drink at the weekend and after 5 p.m. They use alcohol to cope with daily life, but it's a delicate balance. They drink little, regularly. Not so much as to cause problems but enough to be on first-name terms with the guy who runs the off-licence.

Actual footage of you pouring a small drink

O'clock

Adults often say 'o'clock' after the names of alcoholic drinks as a way of making light of their alcohol dependency. All over the land on Friday at 4 p.m., you can hear cries of 'It's nearly wine o'clock!' or 'It's nearly gin o'clock!' Hilarious.

What they mean is that it's nearly time to drag themselves home, open a bottle of wine and down the lot, while binging on Friday-night TV.

5 p.m.

Beer o'clock

6 p.m.

Gin o'clock

10 p.m.

Shots o'clock

2 a.m.

Vomit o'clock

Biggest lies we tell ourselves

#5

JUST A QUIET ONE TONIGHT

Biggest lies we tell ourselves

#6

I'M NEVER DRINKING AGAIN

Pretending to enjoy wine

Many adults pretend to know about wine and many more pretend to enjoy it. The popularity of prosecco and the fact that it's the wine that most resembles fizzy pop shows how much everyone is really bluffing at adulting.

Pairing wine with food is a great way to adult. As a general rule, white wine goes with delicate dishes like fish, while red wine goes with robust meals like steak and curry. Don't even try to pair rosé with food. Real adults don't touch the stuff.

Alcohol choices by age

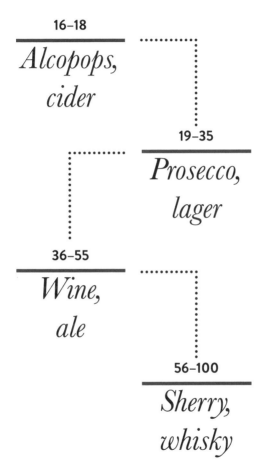

16–18
Alcopops, cider

19–35
Prosecco, lager

36–55
Wine, ale

56–100
Sherry, whisky

What the wine list says	What the wine list means
Vintage	It's not really old, but it *is* really expensive. Vintage wine uses grapes that were picked in a single year
Tannins	The taste in red wine that dries your mouth out
Terroir	A sense of place, where the grapes are from, climate and soil type. It's made-up nonsense for people with more money than sense
Dry	Don't worry, the wine is still wet, but it tastes 'dry'
13% Alc/Vol	This denoted the amount of alcohol in the wine. If you go too strong (over 14 per cent) you will end up with purple teeth and a banging headache

Ordering wine

A restaurant wine list is a daunting thing full of words you don't understand and terms you've never seen before. As a rule of thumb, most adults order the second cheapest bottle in the colour of wine they prefer. The cheapest would insinuate that they are a cheapskate, and more expensive wines are too much of a risk.

When the wine arrives, taste the wine but don't compliment the waiter on the taste. They didn't make it and are only waiting for you to confirm whether the wine is corked or not. Wine that is corked smells and tastes really bad.

Moderation and keeping your dignity

If you are planning to drink more than the recommended daily allowance then you must remember to eat before you drink. A full stomach means you absorb alcohol slower.

Not eating before drinking also increases the likelihood of eating late-night fast food and passing out in your own vomit. Learning to call it a night becomes harder the more you drink, as your judgement is impaired.

Don't say	Do say
Let's do shots!	Nightcap?
Let's go for a kebab!	Cheese and biscuits?
I'm completely bollocksed	No more for me, I'm a bit squiffy
Down in one!	This wine really is quaffable
The club is open until 4 a.m., let's go fucking mental	I'm afraid its an early night for me, I've got a supermarket delivery scheduled for 6.30 a.m.

WINE BEFORE BEER

Oh dear

BEER BEFORE WINE

Nice time*

*Disclaimer: not true

Hangovers

The inevitable outcome of drinking is a hangover. As you get older hangovers get worse. A hangover for a twenty-one-year-old consists of an inconvenient headache and a mild sense of regret. A thirty-one-year-old experiences pain beyond measure, a longing for the welcome embrace of death, and an all-encompassing feeling of remorse.

Coping strategies for hangovers include:

1. Hydration, relaxation and nutrition
Drink water, sleep, and eat healthily if you can hold it down. Your body needs hydration, sugar and rest.

2. Hair of the dog
Drink more. You can't have a hangover if you are still drunk. This is, of course, very ill-advised.

3. Don't drink too much in the first place
The ultimate cure, but one of the hardest to achieve.

I've got hair of the dog, and face.

Hangover cure recipes

Aspirin

Water, aspirin

Prairie Oyster

Egg yolk,
Worcestershire
sauce, Tabasco

Bloody Mary

Tomato juice,
vodka,
Worcestershire
sauce, Tabasco

Coffee

Coffee

The morning after drinking when you are twenty-one

The morning after drinking
when you are thirty-one

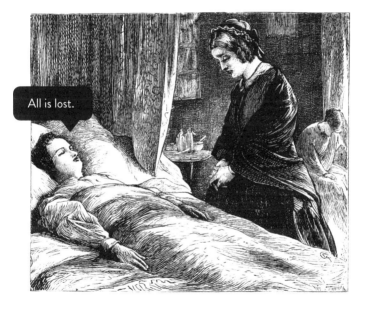

DRINK MORE WATER

DRINK LESS BOOZE

Afterword

Success!

If you follow the advice in this book you will give yourself a better chance at adulting.

As we will all be dead in a ditch before we know it, it's also important to do what makes you happy and try not to grow up too much in the adulting process. Even the most adulty adults will have a secret childish nature to them, somewhere.

After successfully adulting for one day

Rewards

Remember to reward yourself with a treat when you have successfully adulted. Cut out a reward and wear it with pride every time you adult!

Adults say:

CARPE DIEM

'Seize the day'

Non-adults say:

YOLO

'You only live once'

About the author

Stephen Wildish is the author of *How to Swear: An illustrated guide*. He's also an idiot. An idiot who is barely adulting himself. His advice should be taken with a large, adult-sized pinch of salt.

Stephen studied Fine Art at Sheffield Hallam University (where he learned skills he has not used once) and now runs a design studio in Marlborough, Wiltshire.

Stephen is the current 100m Sack race world record holder.

Jake Allnutt

Matthew Croston

Dan Gleeballs

Verity Halliday

Jamie Stapleton

Susan Wildish

Being an adult is just
googling how to do things.

10

Pop Press, an imprint of Ebury Publishing
20 Vauxhall Bridge Road
London SW1V 2SA

Pop Press is part of the Penguin Random House group of companies whose
addresses can be found at global.penguinrandomhouse.com

Copyright © Stephen Wildish 2018

Stephen Wildish has asserted his right to be identified as the author of this
Work in accordance with the Copyright, Designs and Patents Act 1988

First published in the United Kingdom by Pop Press in 2018

www.penguin.co.uk

A CIP catalogue record for this book is available from the British Library

ISBN 9781529102536

Printed and bound in TBB, a.s. Slovakia

Penguin Random House is committed to a sustainable future
for our business, our readers and our planet.
This book is made from Forest Stewardship Council® certified paper.